INITIAL QUIZZES

First published in 2002 by Miles Kelly Publishing Ltd,
Bardfield Centre, Great Bardfield, Essex, CM7 4SL

ISBN 1-84236-133-3

2 4 6 8 10 9 7 5 3

Project Manager: Ian Paulyn
Assistant: Lisa Clayden
Design: Clare Sleven

Contact us by email: info@mileskelly.net
Website: www.mileskelly.net

Printed in India

INITIAL QUIZZES

by
Christopher Rigby

Miles Kelly
PUBLISHING

About the Author

Born in Blackburn, Lancashire in 1960, Christopher Rigby has been compiling and presenting pub quizzes for the past 15 years. When he is not adding to his material for quizzes, Christopher works in the car industry. He is married to Clare – they have two teenage daughters, Hollie and Ashley and share their home with two demented dogs called Vespa and Bailey. A keen Manchester United fan Christopher lists his heroes as George Best and Homer Simpson.

INITIAL QUIZZES EXPLAINED

This quiz book comprises 90 sets of quizzes. The initials to each answer are given before the start of each question. This may enable you to work out the answer, or make a reasonable guess.

Five example questions are set out below:

1. The M of V – In which play does Shylock demand a pound of flesh? (*The Merchant of Venice*)

2. M R – Who owned the Magic Roundabout? (Mr Rusty)

3. P F – In which film does John Travolta play the character of Vincent Vega? (*Pulp Fiction*)

4. W P – Who founded the city of Philadelphia? (William Penn)

5. G and S – Who wrote the Savoy Operas? (Gilbert & Sullivan)

QUIZ ONE

....

1. T J – What name is given to a pottery mug depicting a stout man usually dressed in 18th-century garb?

2. B W – Which species of female spider kills the male after mating?

3. O G – What nickname is given to the American Stars and Stripes flag?

4. S the C – What charity was founded in 1919 by a certain Miss Jebb?

5. A P – What name for an occupation is French for 'on an equal basis'?

6. F D – What is the name of the legendary ghost ship which is allegedly sighted off the coast of Africa during bad weather?

7. A of the C – Which object supposedly contained the tablets on which the Ten Commandments were inscribed?

8. P W – What is the alternative name for a coyote?

9. T E – What occurred in the UK on August 11th 1999?

10. The P is M T the S – Which famous saying is attributed to a gentleman by the name of Bulwer-Lytton?

ANSWERS

1. Toby Jug 2. Black widow 3. Old Glory 4. Save the Children 5. Au pair 6. Flying Dutchman 7. Ark of the Covenant 8. Prairie wolf 9. Total Eclipse 10. The pen is mightier than the sword

QUIZ TWO

1. G B – Where in the human body is bile stored?
2. Y G – How should one formally address an archbishop?
3. B P H – What is the name of the headquarters of the Boy Scout's association?
4. H C – Red Connors was the sidekick of which Wild West hero?
5. M G – What do those initials stand for in the motoring world?
6. G R Y M G – In a Christmas carol what line comes before 'Let nothing you dismay'?
7. The O of L – What is the name of the highest military decoration in the Soviet Union?
8. M C – According to legend which animal lost its tail when it was trapped in the doors of Noah's Ark?
9. A K – What name is given to the ruler of a Shi-ite Muslim sect?
10. The U B B – Which social event reached its conclusion when the ants danced with the bees?

QUIZ THREE

1. K D – What is the world's largest lizard?
2. M A – Which street is the centre of the advertising industry in New York?
3. The R at the E of the U – What was the sequel called to *The Hitchhiker's Guide To The Galaxy*?
4. T T T – What do they call noughts and crosses in the USA?
5. The F L – What was founded by a Frenchman called Louis Philippe?
6. B H – What is the name of the headquarters of the BBC World Service?
7. D I D – 'By the Sleepy Lagoon' is the theme tune to which radio show?
8. J F – Which detective lives at Cabot Cove in the American state of Maine?
9. P M – Who is the sponsor of the tallest rollercoaster in Europe?
10. H D – What is the alternative name for leprosy?

QUIZ FOUR

1. The T D A – Which law came into being on November 30th 1968?

2. S E – In the movie world what does a foley artist add to the film?

3. G S – What is the ruling body of the Church of England called?

4. L B – What was the very first product to be made by the Philips company?

5. M S – Which successful stage musical is set in Vietnam?

6. L of the V – What is the national flower of Sweden?

7. The C of the L B – What took place on October 25th 1854?

8. C D G – Which foreign phrase when translated into English literally means 'finishing stroke'?

9. T P – By what name is magnesium silicate more commonly known?

10. C D S – What was held for the first time in 1891 in Islington?

ANSWERS

1. The Trade Descriptions Act 2. Sound effects 3. General Synod 4. Light bulbs 5. *Miss Saigon* 6. Lily of the Valley 7. The Charge of the Light Brigade 8. *Coup de grace* 9. Talcum powder 10. Cruft's dog show

QUIZ FIVE

1. T and T – What was the title of the warts-and-all documentary featuring Elton John?
2. N H – Name the actress who played Sandra in *The Liver Birds*?
3. U F – Who did Jackie Coogan play in *The Addams Family*?
4. D of D G – Which long-running TV series was based on the film *The Blue Lamp*?
5. N S S P U N – What is the motto of the BBC?
6. C I – Where does Father Ted live?
7. H M – Which series is set in the Scottish village of Lochdubh?
8. The S of S F – Where did Detective Mike Stone do his detecting?
9. W F G – Which series is set at the Bayview Retirement Home?
10. I C B S G F Y – What is the title of the theme music to *Minder*?

QUIZ SIX

1. B F and M – What were the first words spoken by God to man in the Bible?
2. K C – Which police force was created by Mack Sennett?
3. U P – What was the name of the father of King Arthur?
4. V L – What does the musical term *fortissimo* mean?
5. The J C F C – Under what name did Julian Clary first perform on television?
6. A E – What is advertised on TV with the slogan 'That'll do nicely Sir'?
7. S L – In the animal kingdom what is the alternative name for the ounce?
8. F V – What are the only two words to appear on the Victoria Cross?
9. H S of W and W – Which school is attended by Harry Potter?
10. H F – By what name is pollinosis more commonly known?

QUIZ SEVEN

1. R R – In the USA they call them beltways. What are they called in the UK?
2. The W P – What is the much shorter name for the Eastern European Mutual Assistance Treaty?
3. The C R – What is the name of the famous winter sports course located at St Moritz?
4. A Y L I – Which Shakespeare play features a clown called Touchstone?
5. H T – Which song from the musical *South Pacific* went on to become a No. 1 hit in 1982?
6. N M – Whose autobiography is entitled *The Long Walk To Freedom*?
7. The P of V – Which building houses the famed Hall of Mirrors?
8. J C – Who wrote the novel *Hollywood Wives*?
9. P P – Which horse won the Grand National in 1992?
10. T S N B F W – What is the ninth commandment?

QUIZ EIGHT

1. G M B – What is the title of the sequel to *Gentlemen Prefer Blondes*?

2. K G – In which film did Elvis Presley play a boxer?

3. L T A – From which organization was David Lloyd sacked in the year 2000?

4. A C – What do the initials A C mean to an electrician?

5. T T – By what nickname was the diminutive Charles Sherwood Stratton better known?

6. B and F – What is the motto of the Salvation Army?

7. H C M C – What did Saigon change its name to?

8. C S – What is the acting name of Carlo Estevez?

9. W M – Who was the Vice-President to Jimmy Carter?

10. S M – What is the world's oldest republic?

ANSWERS

1. *Gentlemen Marry Brunettes* 2. *Kid Galahad* 3. Lawn Tennis Association 4. Alternating current 5. Tom Thumb 6. Blood and fire 7. Ho Chi Minh City 8. Charlie Sheen 9. Walter Mondale 10. San Marino

QUIZ NINE

1. N K U – What is the motto of the department store John Lewis?

2. G N – Who was the best man at the wedding of David Beckham and Victoria Adams?

3. K D – Who was granted the freedom of the city of Liverpool in May 2001?

4. F G – By what name is iron pyrites also known?

5. J P – Who was the first woman to train the winner of a Grand National?

6. N E – In April 2001 which show business personality shaved off his 30-year-old beard?

7. K N – What was the name of the disc jockey who was sacked after selling topless photos of Sophie Rhys-Jones to the *Sun* newspaper?

8. The E S C – What did Estonia win in May 2001?

9. G K – Who was voted the Most Glamorous Woman Ever by the woman's magazine Journal?

10. F L A B S L A B – How did Muhammed Ali describe his fighting style?

QUIZ TEN

1. H W – What do the initials H W stand for when a batsman in cricket is given out?

2. D R – In 1977 who was banned from British football for ten years?

3. B the D – Which horse won the Epsom Derby in 1997?

4. C K B – Who unsuccessfully started the Grand National in 1993?

5. L M – Who did Sammy McIlroy succeed as the manager of Northern Ireland?

6. V H – On what might you see a tsukahara performed?

7. J P – Who was the oldest player to compete in the final stages of the 2001 World Snooker Championships?

8. B C – Who was the captain of the American Ryder Cup Team in 1999?

9. D B – Who did *Wisden's Almanac* name as the greatest cricketer of the 20th century?

10. J R – Who was the last English manager of the 20th century to manage an F A Cup winning side?

QUIZ ONE

1. C E of the F K – What phrase describes direct contact with an alien or a UFO?

2. S of the D – What is the name of the official fan club of Laurel and Hardy named after one of their films?

3. M O – Found in the kitchen, what was invented by Percy Spencer?

4. W S J – What is the best-selling daily newspaper in the USA?

5. T S – Who was voted Footballer of the Year in England in 2001?

6. W D – What is the final stage in the life of a star called?

7. The M W K T M – Which film directed by Alfred Hitchcock featured the song 'Que Sera, Sera'?

8. E F – Which Hollywood legend's autobiography was entitled *My Wicked, Wicked Ways*?

9. E and M S – Name the famous couple who married on June 3rd 1937.

10. The S W S C – Which very large group of singers topped the UK singles charts in the Christmas of 1980?

ANSWERS

1. Close encounter of the fourth kind 2. Sons of the Desert 3. Microwave oven 4. *Wall St Journal* 5. Teddy Sheringham 6. White dwarf 7. *The Man Who Knew Too Much* 8. Errol Flynn 9. Edward and Mrs Simpson 10. The Saint Winifred's School Choir

QUIZ TWO

1. P A – Who stood down as leader of the Liberal Party in 1999?

2. M F – Who married both André Previn and Frank Sinatra?

3. R P – Name the actor who died in October 1993 aged just 22.

4. J H – Who wrote the novel *Goodbye Mr Chips*?

5. S F F – Which Lennon and McCartney song was covered by a group called Candy Flip in 1990?

6. N S N A – In which James Bond film did Rowan Atkinson play a bumbling civil servant?

7. A the H – Who was nicknamed 'The Scourge of God'?

8. S S – In the 2001 elections which was the first constituency to return their final voting results?

9. A F – What was the name of the character played by Eddie Murphy in the *Beverley Hills Cop* films?

10. F M – Who sailed around the world in 1519?

ANSWERS

1. Paddy Ashdown 2. Mia Farrow 3. River Phoenix 4. James Hilton 5. 'Strawberry Fields Forever' 6. *Never Say Never Again* 7. Attila the Hun 8. Sunderland South 9. Axel Foley 10. Ferdinand Magellan

QUIZ THREE

1. M M – Who was the first ever person to sing a Bond theme?
2. L D – What is the alternative name for a polygraph machine?
3. G C – What is the name of the scientific instrument that measures radioactivity levels?
4. A of a T D – In which 1970 film did Richard Burton play Henry VIII?
5. C L – Who wrote the sitcoms *Bread* and *Butterflies*?
6. S D – Which film starring Gwyneth Paltrow saw the directorial debut of Peter Howitt?
7. D L I P – What are undoubtedly the most famous four words spoken in the African village of Ujiji?
8. E E – Who replaced Michael Faraday on the back of a £20 note?
9. D F – What was the title of the John Lennon album that was in the charts at the time of his tragic death?
10. E C A – The war film *The Dambusters* was based on which novel?

ANSWERS

1. Matt Munro 2. Lie detector 3. Geiger counter 4. *Anne Of A Thousand Days*
5. Carla Lane 6. *Sliding Doors* 7. Dr Livingstone, I presume? 8. Edward Elgar
9. *Double Fantasy* 10. *Enemy Coast Ahead*

QUIZ FOUR

1. D W – What name is given to a lift in a restaurant used to transport food?
2. J M – Name the British actor who died on July 23rd 1984.
3. The Y O – Who represented Scumbag College on University Challenge?
4. B B – She was born Camille Javal and she was one of the world's top sex symbols in the 1960s. Who is she?
5. B E – Who was Cilla Black's first manager?
6. S S – Which popular children's TV series made its TV debut in America in November 1969?
7. R M – What does a omophagic creature eat?
8. S T – Who was the pilot of *Thunderbird 1*?
9. W D – What do the initials W D represent when they appear on a netball shirt?
10. T H – Name the Poet Laureate who died in October 1998.

ANSWERS

1. Dumb waiter 2. James Mason 3. The Young Ones 4. Brigitte Bardot 5. Brian Epstein 6. *Sesame Street* 7. Raw meat 8. Scott Tracy 9. Wing defence 10. Ted Hughes

QUIZ FIVE

1. K S – Who did Prince Andrew romance in 1982, much to the displeasure of his mother?

2. L B – Which famous name from the world of show-business was born Diane Belmont?

3. F M – What was the name of the Scottish heroine who assisted in the escape of Bonnie Prince Charlie in 1746?

4. M M – Who had a UK No. 1 hit in 1990, with the song 'Show Me Heaven'?

5. V W – Name the famous fashion designer who opened a shop called 'Nostalgia of Mud'.

6. C of W – What title did Sophie Rhys-Jones receive after her marriage to Prince Edward?

7. C K – Who was Radio Caroline named after?

8. E F – Who was nicknamed 'The First Lady of Song'?

9. C S – Which actress was voted Rear of the Year in 2001?

10. G J – In 1980 who famously slapped Russell Harty during a TV interview?

ANSWERS
1. Koo Stark 2. Lucille Ball 3. Flora Macdonald 4. Maria McKee 5. Vivienne Westwood
6. Countess of Wessex 7. Caroline Kennedy 8. Ella Fitzgerald 9. Claire Sweeney
10. Grace Jones

20

QUIZ SIX

1. K E – Whose only Top 10 hit single came in 1983 courtesy of a song called 'Snot Rap'?

2. The A of Y – Which man of the cloth signs his letters with the word Ebor?

3. S O M M W S – What was the title of the film in which a former TV 'Golden Girl' played the mother of Sylvester Stallone?

4. T W – Who beat Frank Bruno when he fought for the world title for the first time?

5. The K O F – What is the name of the regiment that features in the TV drama *Soldier, Soldier*?

6. B P in the C – What was the title of the sequel to the children's film *Babe*?

7. A of B – Which was the third Swedish group to have a UK No. 1 hit single?

8. W S – What is a penang lawyer?

9. H to M A M – In which 1953 film was Marilyn Monroe desperately searching for a wealthy husband?

10. N V – What was the title of the TV sketch show in which the character of Rab C Nesbitt first appeared?

ANSWERS

1. Kenny Everett 2. The Archbishop of York 3. *Stop Or My Mom Will Shoot* 4. Tim Witherspoon 5. The King's Own Fusiliers 6. *Babe, Pig In The City* 7. Ace of Bass 8. Walking stick 9. *How To Marry A Millionaire* 10. *Naked Video*

QUIZ SEVEN

1. N O – Which American city acquired the nickname of 'The Birthplace of Jazz'?

2. A C V – An ACV is a type of hovercraft. What do those initials stand for?

3. F M – Who captained Arsenal FC when they won the double in 1971?

4. The P A R T – Which novel by James Cain became a film starring Jack Nicholson?

5. Y N W A – Which famous anthem featured in the musical *Carousel* and went on to become a No. 1 hit in 1963?

6. B G – What was the name of the arch that used to separate East Berlin from West Berlin?

7. G G – Who led the Dambusters' raid in World War II?

8. C the R – What is a dromophobic person afraid of doing?

9. D D M – Who wrote the novel *Jamaica Inn*?

10. S B – What is eugenics the study of?

ANSWERS

1. New Orleans 2. Air-cushioned vehicle 3. Frank McClintock 4. *The Postman Always Rings Twice* 5. 'You'll Never Walk Alone' 6. Brandenberg Gate 7. Guy Gibson 8. Crossing the road 9. Daphne du Maurier 10. Selective breeding

QUIZ EIGHT

....

1. R D – What was the call sign of Kris Kristofferson in the film *Convoy*?

2. B M – Which famous name from the world of pop music died on May 11th 1981?

3. H M – Who starred in her first film *Tiger Bay* when she was just 12 years old?

4. I R – What was founded by Chris Blackwell?

5. F L – *Song Without End* is a film biography chronicling the life of which composer?

6. I S C – Who was Larry Grayson's female partner in *The Generation Game*?

7. W N S – What is the motto of the detective agency Pinkerton's?

8. R C – How is Philippe Pages better known when he is playing the piano?

9. S B – On January 30th 1983 it became compulsory to wear what in the UK?

10. H M – In 1997 who was voted Sexiest Woman on TV by *Radio Times* readers?

QUIZ NINE

1. S O H – Which famous building was designed by Jorn Utzon?

2. T the H R - Which soap opera is set in the Scottish village of Glendarroch?

3. A and E – In which medical drama does Martin Shaw play Dr Knutsford?

4. P P M – What was the title of the Beatles' debut album?

5. B H – Who became chairman of Leyton Orient FC in 1995?

6. D W – Who married Alice Fitzwarren?

7. D or A – Pete Burns was the lead singer of which 80s chart-topping group?

8. The B of A – Which film told the true story of Robert F Stroud?

9. The S in the S – Which Disney animated feature told the story of King Arthur when he was a boy?

10. B R – What piece of sporting equipment used to be called a battledore?

ANSWERS

1. Sydney Opera House 2. Take The High Road 3. Always and Everyone 4. Please Please Me 5. Barry Hearn 6. Dick Whittington 7. Dead or Alive 8. The Birdman Of Alcatraz 9. The Sword In The Stone 10. Badminton racquet

QUIZ TEN

1. J L J J – Which 1990 hit record was about a man killed by Bob Ford?

2. J W – Who topped the charts in the Christmas of 1986 two years after his death?

3. S O – What was the title of John Lennon's first solo No. 1 hit?

4. The P S – In the world of pop music how are Anita, Bonnie and June collectively known?

5. O N in B – Which song from the stage show *Chess* provided Murray Head with a hit record?

6. M M – What is the title of the stage musical that features 28 hit songs by Abba and is named after one of their No. 1 hits?

7. B M – Who let the dogs out?

8. W Y W – Which Status Quo hit was used in a TV advert for the high-street chain Argos?

9. D Y T I S – What did Rod Stewart ask in the title of a 1978 No. 1 hit?

10. L S A L – What was the title of the song which won the Eurovision Song Contest for Katrina and the Waves?

ANSWERS

1. 'Just Like Jesse James' 2. Jackie Wilson 3. 'Starting Over' 4. The Pointer Sisters 5. 'One Night In Bangkok' 6. *Mamma Mia* 7. Baha Men 8. 'Whatever You Want' 9. 'Do Ya Think I'm Sexy' 10. 'Love Shine A Light'

QUIZ ONE

....

1. L S – By what name is Paul O'Grady known as when he dons a blonde wig?

2. F A – Who sang the song 'Beauty School Dropout' in the film *Grease*?

3. G S - Who was nicknamed 'The Father of the Railway'?

4. A A E – Which pop group took their name from the title of a 1950 film starring Bette Davis?

5. The T D F – Which famous race was first contested in 1903?

6. H C A – Whose autobiography is entitled *The Tale of My Life*?

7. E R – Who found her '15 minutes of fame' when she streaked at Twickenham in 1982?

8. The L U – The famous map of the what was designed by a gentleman called Harry Beck in the 1930s?

9. The B to P – In the Muslim faith what is the Alsirat?

10. L P – What is the world's highest capital city?

ANSWERS

1. Lily Savage 2. Frankie Avalon 3. George Stephenson 4. All About Eve 5. The Tour de France 6. Hans Christian Andersen 7. Erica Roe 8. The London underground 9. The Bridge to Paradise 10. La Paz

26

QUIZ TWO

1. Q L – Dr Sam Beckett is the lead character in which TV series?
2. The S of S – What nickname was given to the serial killer David Berkowitz?
3. A D W D – Which song opens with the line 'I close my eyes, draw back the curtains'?
4. The S of L – Which famous landmark can be seen on Bedloe's Island?
5. J B – Who made news headlines in 1992 when he was photographed kissing the toes of Sarah Ferguson?
6. F I W A I W P – What are the first seven words in the lyrics of the song 'I Will Survive'?
7. K F – Crane, dragon and tiger are all styles of what?
8. J D – Name the singer who died in a plane crash in 1997.
9. O F T – A figure of who appears on the weathercock at Lords Cricket Ground?
10. W H – Who resigned on the 8th June 2001?

ANSWERS

1. *Quantum Leap* 2. The Son of Sam 3. 'Any Dream Will Do' 4. The Statue of Liberty 5. John Bryan 6. First I was afraid I was petrified 7. Kung Fu 8. John Denver 9. Old Father Time 10. William Hague

QUIZ THREE

1. T R – Which 1990 film was advertised with the publicity blurb 'They stole his mind, now he wants it back'?

2. U P – On which No. 1 song did Queen collaborate with David Bowie?

3. G V – Who was shot dead in Miami in July 1997?

4. A M – Which Spanish football club was managed by Ron Atkinson?

5. J I – Who was the first ever chief executive of Channel 4?

6. F B – The film *Funny Girl* told the story of the life of which entertainer?

7. J D – In *Coronation Street* who was Don Brennan's best man when he married Ivy?

8. N D I B – What is the title of the theme song to the James Bond film *The Spy Who Loved Me*?

9. J D – Who was America's first ever Public Enemy Number One?

10. The T of L – Where does the Ceremony of the Keys take place at 9.40 p.m. every evening?

QUIZ FOUR

1. The L T of P – Which famous landmark contains 296 steps?

2. N L – Who played the son of Ronnie Barker in the sitcom *Going Straight* and the son of Wendy Craig in the sitcom *Butterflies*?

3. The I R C – Which organization won the only Nobel Peace Prize to be awarded during World War I?

4. C L – In 1990 which athlete published his autobiography which was entitled *Inside Track*?

5. B N – What is studied by a caliologist?

6. J R – Which singer was nicknamed 'The Sultan of Sob'?

7. T W – Which singer had a No. 1 hit in May 1975 and died in April 1998?

8. E M – What was the name of the suffragette who died under the King's horse in the 1913 Derby?

9. B C C – Dr Marie Stopes opened Britain's first what?

10. N Y K – What was the name of the first ever recognized baseball team?

ANSWERS
1.The Leaning Tower of Pisa 2. Nicholas Lyndhurst 3. The International Red Cross 4. Carl Lewis 5. Bird's nests 6. Johnny Ray 7. Tammy Wynette 8. Emily Davidson 9. Birth Control Clinic 10. New York Knickerbockers

QUIZ FIVE

1. O N – What connects the retina to the brain?
2. B P – What is lowered by a beta blocker?
3. G P – If you were experiencing horipitulation what would your body be covered with?
4. S C – What is the more common name for a malignant melanoma?
5. G M – What is the technical name for the largest muscle in the human body?
6. W H – Who is credited with the discovery of the circulation of the blood?
7. A L – Prosthetics is the making of what?
8. A G – Addison's disease is caused by a failure of the what?
9. I O H E F Y – What was the title of Art Garfunkel's 1975 No. 1 hit?
10. J M – Who, portrayed on film by John Hurt, suffered from neurofibromatosis?

QUIZ SIX

1. R the W – Complete the following saying, 'The hand that rocks the cradle..........'.

2. S F – What is the name of the restaurant partly owned by Bill Wyman and named after the title of a Rolling Stones album?

3. L Y – Who was the only goal-keeper to be voted European Footballer of the Year in the 20th century?

4. The B B – He was born J P Richardson and he died in a plane crash. What was the stage name of this singer?

5. C S – What breed of dog was Lady in the Disney animation *Lady And The Tramp*?

6. N B – What is the name of the ventriloquist doll operated by Roger de Courcey?

7. The A D – By what nickname is the character of Jack Dawkins known in a famous novel?

8. L I B – What was the title of the Beatles' last single released whilst they were still together?

9. M and M G – The song 'The Sun Has Got Its Hat On' featured in which musical?

10. I W to B F – A video for which song featured Freddie Mercury vacuuming his living room whilst dressed in a black leather mini skirt?

QUIZ SEVEN

1. I S A – What do those initials stand for in the world of banking?
2. F B – Where was Sergeant Bilko based?
3. S L – Which was the first city outside of Europe to host the Summer Olympic Games?
4. S W – Who played the title role in the film *Young Winston*?
5. B and the B – What was the first ever animated film to be nominated for a Best Film Oscar?
6. C M – In 1995 which British driver won the World Rally Driver's Championships?
7. H L – Who competed in the 1980 Oxford and Cambridge boat race and went on to become a famous name in the world of entertainment?
8. T T – In the city of Brussels there is a museum and several shops dedicated solely to which cartoon character?
9. W S – On film which actor was Passenger 57?
10. J W – Who was the first athlete to run 100 sub four minute miles?

ANSWERS
1. Individual Savings Account 2. Fort Baxter 3. St Louis 4. Simon Ward 5. *Beauty And The Beast* 6. Colin McCrae 7. Hugh Laurie 8. Tin Tin 9. Wesley Snipes 10. John Walker

32

QUIZ EIGHT

1. J R – In 1995 who challenged John Major for the leadership of the Conservative Party?

2. E B – Who connects the films *The Dirty Dozen*, *The Poseidon Adventure* and *Ice Station Zebra*?

3. M H – Which character played on TV by Stacy Keach first appeared in a novel called *I, The Jury*?

4. S L M – What is the name of the peak that overlooks the city of Rio de Janeiro?

5. D M – Name the actor who died of a heart attack in March 1998 aged just 45.

6. A N S in B S – What is the title of the Queen Mother's favorite song?

7. G C - What is the name of the lady who has made a career out of impersonating Queen Elizabeth II?

8. T D W T B O – In which film did Errol Flynn play General Custer?

9. The V I – What are jointly owned by Great Britain and the USA?

10. The I C – What is the title of the first greatest hits album of Madonna?

QUIZ NINE

1. I P – In which film did Robert Redford offer Demi Moore 1 million dollars to sleep with him?

2. S C – Who became the Member of Parliament for Falmouth and Camborne in 1992?

3. The K D – Which famous race celebrated its centenary in 1975?

4. L D – Who created the fictional character of Harry Palmer?

5. G S S – What begins on the August 12th and ends on December 10th?

6. P I – In which film was Harrison Ford accused of the murder of Greta Scacchi?

7. O B - What is the name of the cow in the pantomime *Jack and the Beanstalk*?

8. H S – Which sporting figure's autobiography is entitled *V Is For Victory*?

9. S S – In which sport are competitors required to change lanes after every lap?

10. The F M with the B B – In the sitcom *Allo, Allo* what is the title of the painting that the Resistance are constantly trying to hide from the Germans?

QUIZ TEN

1. W W – What is the name of the Scottish hero portrayed by Mel Gibson in the film *Braveheart*?

2. T A – In the *Toy Story* films who voiced Buzz Lightyear?

3. S E F – What is the title of the 1985 film that is also the name given to the luminous area that can appear around church steeples?

4. L to K – Which Bond theme was performed by Gladys Knight?

5. The P V L F – In which 1996 film did Woody Harrelson play a pornography merchant?

6. B K – Which Oscar-winning film star was born Krishna Banji?

7. A P – What is the title of the 1997 film in which Gene Hackman plays the President of the USA and Clint Eastwood plays a cat burglar?

8. R N – When Alec Guinness played Fagin who played Bill Sykes?

9. T B – What is the title of the 1981 film in which John Cleese played Robin Hood?

10. A the P M – Which 1976 film told the story of the two *Washington Post* journalists who uncovered the Watergate scandal?

ANSWERS

1. William Wallace 2. Tim Allen 3. St Elmo's fire 4. Licence To Kill 5. The People Versus Larry Flynt 6. Ben Kingsley 7. Absolute Power 8. Robert Newton 9. Time Bandits 10. All The President's Men

QUIZ ONE

1. B the B – What was the title of the first UK No. 1 hit single to be sung in Spanish?

2. L B – What was the title of the second UK No. 1 hit single to be sung in Spanish?

3. W W – Who was the daughter of Hippolyte, Queen of the Amazons?

4. Z R – Who is nicknamed 'The Punk Princess of Fashion'?

5. N C – Who was the first gymnast to score a perfect 10?

6. N K – Who was the second gymnast to score a perfect 10?

7. P H – Which actress played the title role in the TV drama *Jemima Shore Investigates*?

8. I B – Who wrote the song 'White Christmas'?

9. Q A – What style of furniture was popular in England in the early 18th century?

10. A W – Who was appointed the Mayoress of Weatherfield in 1973?

QUIZ TWO

1. U R – Who was the narrator of the Brer Rabbit stories?

2. R D – What was the name of the former newsreader who died in December 1999 aged 86?

3. M Y – Which teenage pop group collaborated with Donna Summer on the song 'Unconditional Love'?

4. B B – In which West End musical did Barbara Dickson play Mrs Johnstone?

5. L L – Who was voted BBC Sports Personality of the Year in 1999?

6. B M – Who acquired the nickname of 'The Divine Miss M'?

7. W G – Who links the films *Made In America, Soapdish and Ghost*?

8. S L – Which country played their first ever cricket test match in 1982?

9. B N – Which Grand National winning horse could possibly have been 1343 metres (4,406 feet) high?

10. The C of E – Which Shakespeare play features two pairs of identical twins?

ANSWERS
1. Uncle Remus 2. Robert Dougal 3. Musical Youth 4. *Blood Brothers* 5. Lennox Lewis 6. Bette Midler 7. Whoopi Goldberg 8. Sri Lanka 9. Ben Nevis 10. *The Comedy of Errors*

QUIZ THREE

1. S the G – In the Tolkien novel what was the name of the Lord of the Rings?

2. E W – Who died on March 2nd 1999, fifteen years after his comedy partner?

3. S G – Who wrote the novel *Cold Comfort Farm*?

4. R C – Who was the first singer to have a chart hit with the song 'This Ole House'?

5. M J – In 1999 Luciana Gemenez gave birth to which famous man's love-child?

6. V V – What was the title of the film in which Judge Reinhold and Fred Savage played a father and son who magically exchanged identities?

7. The M of Q – In the world of boxing how is John Sholto Douglas otherwise known?

8. M M – Which former West Indian fast bowler died in 1999 aged 41?

9. U the A – What was the theme song of the comedy duo Flanagan & Allen?

10. B H – Who was sacked from the pop group East 17 for endorsing ecstasy?

QUIZ FOUR

1. T W – Which famous name in the world of sport has the real first name of Eldrick?

2. E A – With which two words did every episode of *Dixon of Dock Green* begin?

3. J T – Which pop group named themselves after the inventor of the seed drill?

4. B and B – With which duo did Cher re-release the song 'I Got You Babe' in 1994?

5. R H – Who did Rod Stewart marry in 1990?

6. B on the R K – Colonel Nicholson was one of the main characters in which Oscar-winning film?

7. W the H I – In which drama series did Sarah Lancashire and Pam Ferris co-star as community nurses?

8. The C of A – What is the name of the organization that oversees British heraldry?

9. E B – Who did Adolph Hitler marry in 1945?

10. The S of K E – In which 1965 western did Dean Martin play the brother of John Wayne?

ANSWERS

1. Tiger Woods 2. 'Evening all' 3. Jethro Tull 4. Beavis and Butthead 5. Rachel Hunter 6. *Bridge On The River Kwai* 7. *Where The Heart Is* 8. The College of Arms 9. Eva Braun 10. *The Sons Of Katie Elder*

4

QUIZ FIVE

....

1. T P A – What is the nickname of New York's 28th Street?

2. O S - Where in London would you find Selfridges?

3. C R – Which country is sandwiched by Nicaragua and Panama?

4. C C – The initials CC can be seen on the watermark of Commonwealth stamps. What do those initials stand for?

5. The F R S – What is the central bank of the USA called?

6. The P G – Where in the world is the sea water the hottest?

7. S A – In which Texan city is the Alamo situated?

8. The S of D – What is in the middle of the flag of Israel?

9. The K P – What connects Afghanistan and Pakistan?

10. S P P – What is the capital of Guernsey?

QUIZ SIX

1. G E – Which famous novel shares its title with the debut album of the singer Tasmin Archer?

2. C B – Which actress played the title role in the 1998 film *Elizabeth*?

3. C of F – Which 1981 film reached its conclusion at the 1924 Paris Olympics?

4. H C – What is the title of the medical drama that is a spin off from *Casualty*?

5. S C – Name the actor who died in 1996 aged 45 and played Jeffrey Fairbrother in the sitcom *Hi-De-Hi*.

6. S P – What is the largest city in Brazil in terms of population?

7. B V – What name is given to the cocktail that consists of Guinness and champagne?

8. D V – What is the name of the hottest desert in the USA?

9. E B – Who created the characters of Orinoco, Tobermory and Uncle Bulgaria?

10. C E – Name the famous sporting personality who paid a fee of £1,000 in order to attain the title of Lord Brighton.

ANSWERS

1. *Great Expectations* 2. Cate Blanchett 3. *Chariots of Fire* 4. *Holby City* 5. Simon Cadell 6. Sao Paulo 7. Black Velvet 8. Death Valley 9. Elizabeth Beresford 10. Chris Eubank

QUIZ SEVEN

1. O D B - What is the title of the sitcom which is set at Hatley Railway Station?
2. G B of F – What is the title of the film biography in which Dennis Quaid played rock and roller Jerry Lee Lewis?
3. T the L G – What is the title of the sequel to *Alice's Adventures In Wonderland*?
4. C B – In which fictional village is Noel's House Party set?
5. B G J – Who founded Motown Records?
6. O O – What code name was given to the allied invasion of Normandy in 1944?
7. G R – Name the legendary dancer who died in April 1995.
8. S of a W – In which film did Al Pacino win an Oscar playing a blind man?
9. I T – What was introduced into the UK in 1986 to replace Capital Transfer Tax?
10. W P – Situated in New York State what is the name of the US military academy?

QUIZ EIGHT

1. S of the L – Which novel by Thomas Harris was adapted into a film which won five Oscars?

2. The G T R – What made news headlines on August 7th 1963?

3. A G – Who was the first woman to ride in the Epsom Derby?

4. B M – Members of whose gang were ruthlessly slaughtered in the St Valentine's Day Massacre?

5. S H – What is the capital of Jersey?

6. D M – Who was known as 'The voice of Wimbledon'?

7. The D S of the M – What was photographed for the first time in 1959 and became the title of a top-selling album in 1973?

8. M O – Who was voted BBC Sports Personality of the Year in 1998?

9. The W of A – What is the literal English translation of the word Kismet?

10. E M D W – What four words often spoken by actors playing Sherlock Holmes were never actually written in any of the Sherlock Holmes novels by Arthur Conan Doyle?

ANSWERS

1. *Silence Of The Lambs* 2. The Great Train Robbery 3. Alex Greaves 4. Bugsy Moran 5. St Helier 6. Dan Maskell 7. The dark side of the Moon 8. Michael Owen 9. The will of Allah 10. 'Elementary, my dear Watson'

QUIZ NINE

1. H R – What is the name of the popular novelist who died in October 1997 aged 81?

2. J D – Name the *Carry On* actor who was born James Smith.

3. C P – Who was the last British Governor of Hong Kong?

4. P F – Who was the first actor to win a posthumous Best Actor Oscar?

5. S W M B O – How did Rumpole of the Bailey refer to his wife?

6. T H – What do the initials TH stand for on an ordnance survey map?

7. B H – When the game show *Call My Bluff* returned to the British TV screen in 1996, who replaced Robert Robinson as the host?

8. G C – What was the rank of Prince Charles when he served in the RAF?

9. The I L – What is the collective name given to the USA's eight oldest universities?

10. A M – What was the title of the short-lived soap opera shown by ITV in 1985, that was dropped from the schedules after just 100 episodes?

ANSWERS

1. Harold Robbins 2. Jim Dale 3. Chris Patten 4. Peter Finch 5. She Who Must Be Obeyed 6. Town hall 7. Bob Holness 8. Group Captain 9. The Ivy League 10. Albion Market

QUIZ TEN

1. I T to the T – What song did Clint Eastwood sing in the film *Paint Your Wagon*?

2. M O D – Which song, originally a hit in 1964 for Doris Day, was reissued in 1987 after featuring in a TV advert for Pretty Polly tights?

3. P to A O F – What was the title of the second song that Cliff Richard sang in the Eurovision Song Contest?

4. I A B – What No. I hit starts with the line 'I thought love was only true in fairy tales'?

5. F M – What is the name of the priest in the Beatles' song *Eleanor Rigby*?

6. I F B B – Which song often heard on the terraces at Upton Park featured in the musical *The Passing Show*?

7. H B – Which song was allegedly written by Paul Simon on a platform at Wigan train station?

8. C O E – What was the best-selling single in the UK in 1982?

9. B O T W – Which No. I hit starts with the line 'When you're weary, feeling small'?

10. P and B – The song 'It Ain't Necessarily So' featured in which musical?

ANSWERS

1. 'I Talk To The Trees' 2. 'Move Over Darling' 3. 'Power To All Our Friends' 4. 'I'm A Believer' 5. Father McKenzie 6. 'I'm Forever Blowing Bubbles' 7. 'Homeward Bound' 8. 'Come On Eileen' 9. 'Bridge Over Troubled Water' 10. *Porgy and Bess*

QUIZ ONE

1. The L is M S – In the Bible how does the 23rd Psalm begin?
2. The N W T – What began on November 20th 1945 and reached it's verdict on August 31st 1946?
3. N A – What was the name of the first ever woman to take a seat in the House of Commons?
4. N H – Who wrote the novel *Fever Pitch*?
5. C J – Name the ex-Liverpool footballer who created the Predator football boot.
6. P D – The Michael Fox Foundation is a charity which was established to find a cure for what?
7. W C – Who did Julia Smith marry in 1994?
8. R M – Who played Barney Rubble in the 1994 film version of *The Flintstones*?
9. C P – Who wrote the song 'Blue Suede Shoes'?
10. A on H – What name is given to the dish of oysters wrapped in bacon?

ANSWERS

1. 'The Lord is my shepherd' 2. The Nuremberg war trials 3. Nancy Astor 4. Nick Hornby 5. Craig Johnstone 6. Parkinson's disease 7. Will Carling 8. Rick Moranis 9. Carl Perkins 10. Angels on Horseback

QUIZ TWO

1. M and K – Which duo provided Stock, Aitken and Waterman with their first No1. hit as record producers?
2. T and J – What name is given to the cocktail that consists of rum, brandy, nutmeg, egg and milk?
3. M N – Which member of Bucks Fizz is related to a famous group of singing sisters?
4. C T – Robben Island is in the bay of which city?
5. G P – Name the actor who played the leader of the A Team, who died in 1994.
6. C M – What name is given to fried noodles on a Chinese restaurant menu?
7. The S of G – How is Lake Tiberias otherwise known?
8. S of S for W – Which ministerial post did John Profumo resign from in 1963?
9. L T – Who played the character of Pamela Lynch in the sitcom *Watching*?
10. T B – Which famous man was a member of a pop group called the Ugly Rumours in the 1970s?

ANSWERS
1. Mel and Kim 2. Tom and Jerry 3. Mike Nolan 4. Cape Town 5. George Peppard 6. Chow Mein 7. The Sea of Galilee 8. Secretary of State for War 9. Liza Tarbuck 10. Tony Blair

QUIZ THREE

1. J J – Which writer features on the back of an Irish £10 note?

2. T B – Name the former England international footballer who was sacked as Coventry's manager in 1992.

3. I P – What murder weapon was used to kill Leon Trotsky?

4. P H – What is the name of the chain of restaurants that was opened by Bruce Willis, Arnold Schwarzenegger and Sylvester Stallone?

5. B B – What does the B B stand for in the name of B B King?

6. L G – Which TV personality is the son-in-law of the movie mogul David Puttnam?

7. E L W – What was the title of the song that topped the charts in 1986 for Nick Berry?

8. The B for C P – What is the name of the American equivalent of Britain's Office of Fair Trading?

9. C M – What was the title of the play that Stephen Fry walked out of in 1995?

10. A I H – What is the title of the autobiography of Jimmy Saville?

QUIZ FOUR

1. B W – What does the word brandy literally mean?

2. A M – Which British footballer won the Golden Boot Award in 1992 as Europe's top goal-scorer?

3. R M F – Which Take That chart-topping single featured vocals by Lulu?

4. O W – Who had an affair with Lord Alfred Douglas that caused a scandal?

5. M C – Name the former Olympic gold medallist who died in June 2001 aged 54.

6. The P of P – What is the better-known title of the Slave of Duty?

7. The R C – Which famous sporting trophy was first contested in June 1927?

8. D F – Name the athlete who won a gold medal at the 1968 Olympics employing a style of high jump that now bears his name.

9. C and C – What is the motto of the Automobile Association?

10. V R – Which comedian topped the UK singles charts in November 1991?

ANSWERS
1. Burnt wine 2. Ally McCoist 3. 'Relight My Fire 4. Oscar Wilde 5. Malcolm Cooper 6. *The Pirates of Penzance* 7. The Ryder Cup 8. Dick Fosbury 9. Courtesy and Care 10. Vic Reeves

QUIZ FIVE

1. T V – What is the name of the Oklahoma bomber who was executed by lethal injection on June 11th 2001?

2. J A – Which former aide of Sarah Ferguson was found guilty of murder in May 2001?

3. T E – Lester Piggott, Sophia Loren and Al Capone were all jailed for which crime?

4. T A – In 1990 which England international footballer was jailed for drink driving?

5. B S – What was the name of the terrorist organization that claimed responsibility for the death of eleven athletes at the 1972 Munich Olympics?

6. J B – Name the famous singer who was jailed in 1988 for firearm and assault charges.

7. W B H – Who did Jack McCall kill in the Wild West?

8. D N – Which convicted murderer lived on Melrose Avenue in Cricklewood?

9. R M – Who died after falling from his yacht on November 5th 1991?

10. D E A – Which crime-fighting body in the USA is known by the initials DEA?

ANSWERS

1. Timothy McVeigh 2. Jane Andrews 3. Tax evasion 4. Tony Adams 5. Black September 6. James Brown 7. Wild Bill Hickock 8. Dennis Nilsen 9. Robert Maxwell 10. Drugs Enforcement Agency.

QUIZ SIX

1. Y A – Who was appointed the leader of the PLO in 1968?

2. S P – Who is Westminster Abbey dedicated to?

3. R W – Who was sent off whilst captaining the England international football team in 1986?

4. K H – Name the chef who wrote a book called *Hot Wok*.

5. L D – Which former Master of the Rolls died in 1999 aged 100?

6. I S – Which breed of dog was crowned Cruft's Supreme Champion in 1999?

7. E P – Who played Caroline Winthrop in *Crossroads* and went on to become a famous stage star?

8. N H – Who was the lead singer of the 1980s band Haircut 100?

9. I C U – What do the letters ICU stand for in a hospital?

10. E M – Name the American athlete who won 121 consecutive races before losing to Danny Harris.

ANSWERS

1. Yasser Arafat 2. Saint Peter 3. Ray Wilkins 4. Ken Hom 5. Lord Denning 6. Irish Setter 7. Elaine Paige 8. Nick Heyward 9. Intensive care unit 10. Ed Moses

QUIZ SEVEN

1. S C – What is the capital of Tenerife?
2. A N – Who wrote a book called *A Life Among Antiques*?
3. E N – Who married John Major's son in 1999?
4. Y C H L – Which song has been a hit for both the Supremes and Phil Collins?
5. B J – Name the two No. 1 hits of 1983, the titles of which had the initials B J.
6. L N – Which 1995 film starring Ted Danson was set in Scotland?
7. C S – What is nicknamed Jewish penicillin?
8. G S I – What was the title of the sitcom of yesteryear set in the RAF and starring Robert Lindsay and Tony Selby?
9. G I – What name is given to the playing area in American football?
10. K O – In which village is the soap *Crossroads* set?

ANSWERS

1. Santa Cruz 2. Arthur Negus 3. Emma Noble 4. 'You Can't Hurry Love' 5. 'Billie Jean' and 'Baby Jane' 6. *Loch Ness* 7. Chicken soup 8. *Get Some In* 9. Grid iron 10. King's Oak

QUIZ EIGHT

1. C W – Who won an Oscar for writing the screenplay of *Chariots of Fire*?

2. S G – Who was the first cricketer to score 10,000 runs in Test cricket?

3. N E – What term describes the financial situation whereby a person owes more on a mortgage than their house is worth?

4. A N – Name the former husband of Joan Collins who died in 1999.

5. The W of D – Which famous quote from the Shakespeare play *Richard III* was used to describe the end of 1978 and the beginning of 1979?

6. M R – What is the title of the World War II drama that starred John Thaw as a French Catholic priest?

7. C Z J – The sixth letter of the Greek alphabet forms part of the name of which actress?

8. D B – Name the famous British film star who died in 1999 aged 78.

9. A I – Which organization was awarded a Nobel Peace Prize in 1977?

10. M N – In 1999 which 87-year-old British grandmother was exposed as a former Russian spy?

ANSWERS

1. Colin Welland 2. Sunil Gavaskar 3. Negative equity 4. Anthony Newley 5. The winter of discontent 6. Monsignor Renard 7. Catherine Zeta Jones 8. Dirk Bogarde 9. Amnesty International 10. Melita Norwood

QUIZ NINE

1. P E – What was first published on October 25th 1961?

2. The N L – What took place for the first time in Britain on November 19th 1994?

3. N H – Which glam-rock star made a cameo appearance in the 40th anniversary edition of *Coronation Street*?

4. W D – What song by Elvis Presley topped the UK singles charts in the year that he died?

5. N H – Who did Paul Merton replace as the presenter of the TV show *Room 101*?

6. The M R L P – Alan Hope replaced a lord as the leader of which political party?

7. The I on S – Which British newspaper was launched in January 1990?

8. S D – The autobiography of which painter is entitled *Diary Of A Genius*?

9. C P – When Margaret Thatcher first became prime minister who was the first Tory Party chairman?

10. A S – In a TV advert which famous sports star said 'I'd like a Big Mac, please'?

QUIZ TEN

1. B B – What was heard for the first time in London on New Year's Eve 1923?

2. B N – What is celebrated in Scotland on January 25th?

3. N C – In London what stands 52 metres (170 feet) tall?

4. The B of E – What is nicknamed the Old Lady of Threadneedle Street?

5. W S – Which Roman construction ran from London to Chester?

6. The M S C – What was officially opened in May 1894 by Queen Victoria?

7. P L – What is the alternative name of Middlesex Street in London?

8. R P – Where in London would you find the residence of the American ambassador to the UK?

9. The A of the N - What is the name of the statue that stands just outside Gateshead?

10. T B – Which Scottish bridge is the longest railway bridge in Europe?

ANSWERS

1. Big Ben 2. Burns Night 3. Nelson's Column 4. The Bank of England 5. Watling Street 6. The Manchester Ship Canal 7. Petticoat Lane 8. Regents Park 9. The Angel of the North 10. Tay Bridge

SESSION 6

QUIZ ONE

1. S A – Verulamium was the Roman name for which English city?

2. J G – What was the name of the Mafia crime lord who was found guilty of murder and racketeering in 1992?

3. Y N M – What is the title of the song that was a hit for Boyzone in 1999 and was originally a hit for Anne Murray in 1978?

4. G M – Who trained the famous racehorse Red Rum?

5. S B – Frank Peterson, a German record-producer, is the third husband of which famous singer?

6. S P – What separates Everton's Goodison Park ground from Liverpool's Anfield?

7. P S – Bernard Hedges was the title character in which 70s sitcom?

8. R M – Which famous book-compiler was assassinated in November 1975?

9. M K – Who published his autobiography *True* in the year 2000?

10. J I – Who walked down the aisle with a Man from Uncle and a member of the Magnificent Seven?

QUIZ TWO

1. S L – Name the singer who appeared in several Andrew Lloyd Webber stage productions and died in November 2000 aged 50.

2. C E M – Which song from *The Sound Of Music* was a hit for Shirley Bassey?

3. L M P – Who did Michael Jackson marry in 1994?

4. B P – Which British building announced a mobile phone ban on November 9th 2000?

5. B the B – Who hit No. 1 in the year 2000 with the song 'Can We Fix It'?

6. W W E – Who is credited with inventing the game of rugby?

7. M D – On November 7th 2000 where did the Sweeney foil an attempted diamond robbery?

8. The O G W T – Which TV programme was presented for many years by 'Whispering' Bob Harris?

9. V P – Name the actor who on film played the creator of Edward Scissorhands.

10. The U S – Who is buried beneath the Arc de Triomphe?

ANSWERS

1. Stephanie Lawrence 2. 'Climb Every Mountain' 3. Lisa Marie Presley 4. Buckingham Palace 5. Bob the Builder 6. William Webb Ellis 7. Millennium Dome 8. *The Old Grey Whistle Test* 9. Vincent Price 10. The Unknown Soldier

QUIZ THREE

1. M H – Which android was played on TV by Matt Frewer?

2. G H – Who was the first Chancellor of the Exchequer, in Margaret Thatcher's first Cabinet?

3. M S G – What is the name of the venue in New York that is famous for staging World Championship boxing bouts?

4. The N S – Piers Fletcher Dervish was a character in which sitcom?

5. L N P N S – What were the reputed last words of King Charles II?

6. J J – In a song who formed the impression that Gordon was a moron?

7. A B in the W – Which No. 1 hit contained the line 'Hey teacher, leave those kids alone'?

8. B L – In a film and a book how is William Fisher better known?

9. N M – Who was the first British goalkeeper to be transferred for 1 million pounds?

10. A J – Name the Australian driver who was crowned Formula One World Champion in 1980.

ANSWERS
1. Max Headroom 2. Geoffrey Howe 3. Madison Square Gardens 4. The New Statesman 5. 'Let not poor Nelly starve' 6. Jilted John 7. 'Another Brick In The Wall' 8. Billy Liar 9. Nigel Martyn 10. Alan Jones

QUIZ FOUR

1. J G S – Which actor reprised his film role of Gregory in a belated 1999 sequel called *Gregory's Two Girls*?

2. Z P – In the year 2000 which well-heeled young lady joined the Cheltenham Ladies Hockey Club?

3. S A F – What is the name of the fault in the Earth's crust on which the city of San Francisco is built?

4. P M – Who played Inspector Chisholm in the TV series *Minder*?

5. P M – Who controversially borrowed £373,000 from Geoffrey Robinson?

6. W the S M G – What is the title of the Oasis album that contains the songs 'Wonderwall' and 'Champagne Supernova'?

7. M C – Who was killed by Republicans in 1922 and played on film in 1996 by Liam Neeson?

8. M G – Name the American athlete who set a new world record for the 100 metres in 1999.

9. G R – In June 2001 who was unveiled as the new manager of West Ham United F C ?

10. H of G – What was the title of Blondie's first UK No. 1 hit single?

QUIZ FIVE

1. The W of O – Which famous novel by L Frank Baum was filmed in 1939?

2. A Q on the W F – *The Road Back* was the sequel to which World War I novel?

3. G C – Who was the first ever person to be buried in Poet's Corner?

4. D and S – Which Dickens novel features the character of Polly Toodle?

5. M in the V – What is the title of the story that marked the literary debut of Miss Marple?

6. D L – According to the poem where does the muffin man live?

7. K S M – Name the novel that features the characters of Gagool and Twala?

8. L R – In which town is the novel *The French Lieutenant's Woman* set?

9. G P – In the Beatrix Potter story *The Tale of Tuppenny*, what sort of animal is Tuppenny?

10. E C – Who wrote the novel *A Parliamentary Affair*?

QUIZ SIX

1. K H – In June 2001 who lost her job as Britain's Minister for Sport?

2. V J – Who links the films *Swordfish*, *Gone In 60 Seconds* and *Lock, Stock and Two Smoking Barrels*?

3. The B of I – What nickname is given to the Apennines mountain range?

4. W the C – Who was England's first Norman monarch?

5. B J D – Geri Halliwell sang a cover of the song 'It's Raining Men' for the soundtrack of which film?

6. The W G – What was the name of the duo who had the original hit with the song 'It's Raining Men'?

7. A S – The novel *Robinson Crusoe* was based on the true life adventures of which man?

8. L L – Who starred in the legal drama series *Ally McBeal* and the film version of *Charlie's Angels*?

9. T H – Name the footballer who scored for both sides in the 1981 F A Cup Final.

10. D C – Kelly, Beyonie and Michelle make up which female pop trio?

ANSWERS

1. Kate Hoey 2. Vinnie Jones 3. The Backbone of Italy 4. William the Conqueror 5. *Bridget Jones's Diary* 6. The Weather Girls 7. Alexander Selkirk 8. Lucy Lui 9. Tommy Hutchinson 10. Destiny's Child

QUIZ SEVEN

1. D O – To a darts player what is the madhouse?
2. B F – In which film did Nicole Kidman play Dr Chase Meridian?
3. P M – Name the actress who plays Mrs Doyle in the sitcom *Father Ted*.
4. L H – What is the title of the novel written by James Hilton that is set in the mythical land of Shangri-la?
5. S C – Who took over from Zoe Ball as the presenter of Radio One's breakfast show?
6. A E – Who was named 'The Man of the 20th Century' by *Time* magazine?
7. A D – By what other name is the condition of pre-senile dementia also known?
8. R P – On TV who plays Detective Dave Briggs?
9. K F – When Lucy Lockett lost her pocket who found it?
10. P S – Which famous golfer was killed in a plane crash in 1999?

ANSWERS
1. Double one 2. *Batman Forever* 3. Pauline McLynn 4. *Lost Horizon* 5. Sara Cox 6. Albert Einstein 7. Alzheimer's disease 8. Robert Powell 9. Kitty Fisher 10. Payne Stewart

QUIZ EIGHT

1. H R T – In the medical world what do the initials HRT stand for?

2. M D – On film who did Daniel Hillard become when he dressed as a woman?

3. M M – What is the title of the TV crime drama in which John Nettles plays DCI Barnaby?

4. H P – Who has a pet owl called Hedwig?

5. S D – Name the actress who connects LA Law with the Partridge Family.

6. W I N Y – Which No. I hit contains the line 'Telephone can't take the place of your smile'?

7. E C – Which famous footballer appeared in the 1998 film *Elizabeth*?

8. A C – Name the famous lady who married the archaeologist Sir Max Mallowan.

9. The T W – Jeff Lynne, Tom Petty, Roy Orbison, George Harrison and Bob Dylan formed which band?

10. M H and G H – Name the two English footballers who were members of the Monaco team that won the French title in 1988.

QUIZ NINE

1. B E – Which soap character was infamously resurrected in a Southfork shower?

2. J Q – Name the cyclist who won Britain's first gold medal at the 2000 Sydney Olympics.

3. The S of S L – What was the name of the plane that Charles Lindbergh piloted across the Atlantic Ocean?

4. S and C – Whose last Top 10 hit together was entitled 'All I Ever Need Is You'?

5. C P – Who plays Van Helsing in the film *Dracula 2001*?

6. C C – Name the teenage singing sensation who recorded an album entitled *Voice Of An Angel* in 1999.

7. L V C – In the 1972 film sequel *The Magnificent Seven Ride* who took over the role of Chris from Yul Brynner?

8. J L B – Who is nicknamed 'The Father of Television'?

9. S in S – Name the film in which Tom Hanks played the character of Sam Baldwin.

10. T S and L M – Name the two actors who starred in the film *The Dirty Dozen* and who both went on to top the UK singles charts.

QUIZ TEN

NAME THE FILM STARS WHO CONNECT EACH GROUP OF THREE FILMS.

1. C C – *Fletch, Foul Play* and *The Couch Trip.*
2. S F – *Forrest Gump, Hooper* and *Soapdish.*
3. C L – *Back To The Future, One Flew Over The Cuckoo's Nest* and *Clue.*
4. D H – *Splash, Grumpy Old Men* and *Roxanne.*
5. H K – *The Piano, Sister Act* and *From Dusk Till Dawn.*
6. D W – *Betrayed, Shadowlands* and *An Officer And A Gentleman.*
7. N N – *Cape Fear, The Thin Red Line* and *48 Hours.*
8. G C – *Jagged Edge, Reversal Of Fortune* and *Dangerous Liaisons.*
9. R D – *Tender Mercies, The Godfather* and *Deep Impact.*
10. K B – *Never Say Never Again, Blind Date* and *LA Confidential.*

QUIZ ONE

1. The D of the S V – In the Bible what was performed by Salome?

2. I S – If a meeting is held sub rosa, what does that mean?

3. D H – Which film role was turned down by Frank Sinatra but accepted by Clint Eastwood?

4. G G – Which writer was held captive in her own home by a student over the Easter period in the year 2000?

5. L C – What name is given to an earthed rod placed on top of a tall building?

6. A R – Who wrote the novel *Swallows and Amazons*?

7. T in H – Which song by Eric Clapton was inspired by the tragic death of his son?

8. M S – Name the female sports star who was stabbed in the back in April 1993.

9. M A – What is the alternative name for a rowan tree?

10. The S R – In 1998 Ian Brown served a jail sentence for an air rage incident. Which pop group was he a member of?

ANSWERS

1. The dance of the seven veils 2. In secret 3. *Dirty Harry* 4. Germaine Greer 5. Lightning conductor 6. Arthur Ransome 7. 'Tears in Heaven' 8. Monica Seles 9. Mountain ash 10. The Stone Roses

QUIZ TWO

1. L V – In which film did Jane Horrocks impersonate Shirley Bassey, Barbra Streisand and Gracie Fields?
2. The G B P – Which team won the Superbowl in 1997?
3. K N – Who was found guilty of the M25 murder in the year 2000?
4. C A – Name the real-life actress that Sarah Lancashire portrayed in the TV drama *Seeing Red*.
5. R B – Which former world champion was found guilty of kidnapping his wife and children in February 2000?
6. H C – What is the name of the South African cricket captain who became embroiled in a bribes scandal in the year 2000?
7. A G – Which Scottish goalkeeper did Manchester United sign on loan in 2001?
8. W A W W – What is the title of the only UK No. 1 single for a performer nicknamed 'Satchmo'?
9. G U R – What do the initials GUR stand for with regard to a golf course?
10. The C R – What is the name of the brothel that featured in the film *The Best Little Whorehouse In Texas*?

ANSWERS

1. *Little Voice* 2. The Green Bay Packers 3. Kenneth Noye 4. Coral Atkins 5. Riddick Bowe 6. Hanse Cronje 7. Andy Goram 8. 'What A Wonderful World' 9. Ground under repair 10. The Chicken Ranch

QUIZ THREE

1. M W – Who was crowned World Snooker Champion in the year 2000?

2. C R – Who founded the DeBeers Mining Company?

3. A S – Name the world leader who was assassinated in October 1981.

4. C B – What was the title of the 2000 drama series that told of the love affair between Barbara Windsor and Sid James?

5. D P – Who wrote the song 'I Will Always Love You'?

6. L and L D – In which film did Jane Seymour play a character called Solitaire?

7. J K – Who became the first person to win £1 million on the quiz show *Who Wants To Be A Millionaire*?

8. J D – Finty Williams is the daughter of which actress?

9. J S – Who compered the Miss World pageant in 2001?

10. The S M G O – When Leo Sayer made his *Top of the Pops* debut which song was he singing?

ANSWERS
1. Mark Williams 2. Cecil Rhodes 3. Anwar Sadat 4. *Cor Blimey!* 5. Dolly Parton 6. *Live And Let Die* 7. Judith Keppel 8. Judi Dench 9. Jerry Springer 10. 'The Show Must Go On'

QUIZ FOUR

1. P M – What is the name of the *Daily Mirror* editor who became involved in a shares scandal in the year 2000?

2. C M – Who is the lead singer of Catatonia?

3. F Y – What is the title of the film that saw Mel Gibson age 40 years in one day?

4. N F – Who represented the UK in the 2000 Eurovision Song Contest?

5. H S – What is the name of the gas that emits an aroma of rotten eggs?

6. S D – In which American State is Mount Rushmore found?

7. A G Y G – The song 'There's No Business Like Show Business' featured in which musical?

8. D C – Who won the British Grand Prix in the year 2000?

9. The O B – What is the more popular name for the Central Criminal Court?

10. M D and E – According to Noel Coward who goes out in the midday sun?

ANSWERS

1. Piers Morgan 2. Cerys Matthews 3. *Forever Young* 4. Niki French 5. Hydrogen Sulphide 6. South Dakota 7. *Annie Get Your Gun* 8. David Coulthard 9. The Old Bailey 10. Mad dogs and Englishmen

QUIZ FIVE

1. S J – Name the American general who acquired his nickname after his formidable defence at the Battle of Bull Run.

2. The I M – What is the alternative better-known name of the Sepoy rebellion of the 1850s?

3. The K W – What was ended by the Treaty of Panmunjon?

4. The C W – Which conflict did Britain become involved with in March 1854?

5. V the I - What is the name of the 15th-century prince who is thought to have provided the inspiration for the literary character Count Dracula?

6. The G A – What name is given to the famous speech made by Abraham Lincoln in which he proclaimed that the American government was "Of the people, by the people, for the people"?

7. S P – Who is the only British Prime Minister to have been assassinated?

8. P B – Which postage stamps first featured the portrait of Queen Victoria?

9. And S to B – How did Samuel Pepys conclude his daily diary entries?

10. N and J – Name the famous couple who divorced in 1809.

QUIZ SIX

1. L M – Name the singer who performed at Frank Sinatra's funeral.

2. A in G F – What was the title of the sitcom in which Richard Briers played a vicar?

3. P A – Who sprang to fame wearing a swimsuit whilst playing a character called C J Parker?

4. The B S – Jacqueline Abbot and Briana Corrigan have both been vocalists of which pop group?

5. H B – *The Harder They Fall* was the final screen appearance for which Hollywood legend?

6. A on L – What do those initials stand for with regard to an internet company?

7. D W U – Tony Britton played the father of Nigel Havers in which sitcom?

8. B the W – What is the English translation of the Latin phrase 'Ante bellum'?

9. The G G – Dorothy, Sophia, Rose and Blanche are collectively known as who?

10. R H – Who was the first bowler to take 400 wickets in test cricket?

ANSWERS

1. Liza Minnelli 2. *All In Good Faith* 3. Pamela Anderson 4. The Beautiful South 5. Humphrey Bogart 6. America On Line 7. *Don't Wait Up* 8. Before the war 9. The Golden Girls 10. Richard Hadlee

QUIZ SEVEN

1. The W H F – What nickname is given to the 1923 F A Cup Final, the first to be played at Wembley?

2. D C – Who played on film by John Wayne was born in 1786 and died in 1836?

3. J M – Who owned the holiday camp in *Hi-De-Hi*?

4. S B – How is Princess Aurora otherwise known?

5. Y M of the Y – What title was won by teenager Guy Johnston in the year 2000?

6. A Z – What is the common name given to the temperature of minus 273.15 degrees Centigrade?

7. C C – Who sang the song 'The Best That You Can Do', which was used as the theme for the film *Arthur*?

8. O W I L – In which sitcom did James Bolam, Peter Bowles and Christopher Strauli play hospital patients?

9. J S – Who was the only Englishman to be crowned Snooker World Champion in the 1970s?

10. H K – Who retired as German Chancellor in 1998?

ANSWERS

1. The White Horse Final 2. Davy Crockett 3. Joe Maplin 4. Sleeping Beauty 5. Young Musician of the Year 6. Absolute Zero 7. Christopher Cross 8. Only When I Laugh 9. John Spencer 10. Helmut Kohl

QUIZ EIGHT

1. K P – Which footballer was the top goal-scorer in the English Premiership in the 1999/2000 season?

2. The T W – The Shakespeare play *Troilus and Cressida* is set during which conflict?

3. G C – Who played the character of Arnold in the American sitcom *Different Strokes*?

4. P C – Name the singer who was born Virginia Patterson and who died in 1963.

5. R G – Which famous name in the world of sport married Estelle Cryuff in the year 2000?

6. B R – What is the literal translation into English for the French term *Cordon Bleu*?

7. W G – Tulip, flute and goblet are all types of what?

8. F D and R C – Name the two jockeys who were injured in a plane crash at Newmarket race course in June 2000.

9. F L – Who was the first singer to have three UK No. 1 hits in the same year?

10. D F – Linda and Robert Cochrane were the character names of a married couple in which sitcom?

ANSWERS
1. Kevin Phillips 2. The Trojan War 3. Gary Coleman 4. Patsy Cline 5. Ruud Gullit 6. Blue Riband 7. Wine glass 8. Frankie Dettori and Ray Cochrane 9. Frankie Laine 10. Duty Free

QUIZ NINE

1. The F of the T of K of G and E – In the Bible what were Adam and Eve forbidden to eat?

2. The M B – What was closed down in the year 2000, because it was swinging too much?

3. The W I – Members of which organization heckled Tony Blair on June 7th 2000?

4. A S – Members of which pop group starred in the film *Honest*, directed by Dave Stewart of Eurythmics fame?

5. E C – Rodrigo Diaz de Bivar was better known by which much shorter name?

6. V K the R S – What was the first ever song to be played on MTV?

7. T S H N O G B M – What is the first commandment?

8. T B – Who relinquished the title of Viscount Stansgate?

9. The M A G T M – What is the motto of the Royal Canadian Mounted Police?

10. G K – Who won a Best Supporting Actor Oscar in the film *Cool Hand Luke*?

ANSWERS

1. The fruit of the tree of knowledge of good and evil 2. The Millennium Bridge 3. The Women's Institute 4. All Saints 5. El Cid 6. 'Video Killed The Radio Star' 7. Thou shalt have no other God before me. 8. Tony Benn 9. The Mounties always get their man 10. George Kennedy

QUIZ TEN

1. O A – What is the literal English translation of *Cosa nostra*?
2. N S S – What does *Nessum dorma* mean in English?
3. M E – Which peak took its name from the Greek meaning 'I burn'?
4. M R – What does the German word *Herrenvolk* mean?
5. C M – Which Latin phrase means "of sound mind"?
6. P C – What does Volkswagen mean when translated into English?
7. E T – What is the English translation of the word *Cenotaph*?
8. P P – What does the name of the German pop group Kraftwerk mean in English?
9. W F – What is the literal English meaning of the word *blancmange*?
10. A W – What is the English translation of the German word *Luftwaffe*?

QUIZ ONE

1. The S G – Which was the only group to have three Christmas UK No. I's in the 1990s?

2. M C – In the year 2000 at the age of 67 which actor received a knighthood in the Queen's Birthday Honours list ?

3. G P – What is the name of the Princess Royal's home in the Cotswolds?

4. J E – Which athlete's autobiography is entitled *A Time To Jump*?

5. B F N – What nickname was given to Lester Gillis when he became a gangster?

6. In L M – What was the title of the sitcom in which Thora Hird played an undertaker?

7. R H – Which school was attended by Sandy and Danny in *Grease*?

8. The A C W – What began on April 12th 1861?

9. The M of E D – Which novel was left unfinished by Charles Dickens?

10. The O of the G – Which ceremony celebrated its 650th anniversary in the year 2000?

ANSWERS

1. The Spice Girls 2. Michael Caine 3. Gatcombe Park 4. Jonathan Edwards 5. Baby Face Nelson 6. *In Loving Memory* 7. Rydell High 8. The American Civil War 9. *The Mystery of Edwin Drood* 10. The Order of the Garter

QUIZ TWO

1. S M – Name the former Pakistan cricket captain who received a life ban in the year 2000, for match fixing.
2. C J – In which 1953 film did Doris Day sing 'Secret Love'?
3. J C – He was born James Melgrew. What is the stage name of this comedian?
4. F H B – Who wrote the novel *The Secret Garden*?
5. M Y L – What was the title of the 1970s sitcom in which Barry Evans played the English teacher of a class of foreign students?
6. K L – In which city is the building the Petronas Towers found?
7. D D – Which footballer won his 100th cap for France at Euro 2000?
8. W D the W – The song 'No Matter What', a hit for Boyzone, features in which stage musical?
9. A M – Name the book character who was profoundly in love with Pandora.
10. J W – Watchtower House is the name of the headquarters of which religious group?

QUIZ THREE

1. A D – What is the capital of the United Arab Emirates?

2. R C – Name the singer impersonated by Linford Christie on a celebrity edition of *Stars In Their Eyes*.

3. V C – Who was a founder member of the groups Yazoo and Erasure?

4. I D – What was the title of the 2000 TV drama that starred Ross Kemp as a barrister?

5. C B – With which team did Michael Jordan win six national basketball titles?

6. B the M – According to the old saying, what does travel do?

7. E S – Who illustrated the Winnie the Pooh novels?

8. S W – What is the title of the TV drama in which Amanda Burton plays a police pathologist?

9. A S – What was Darth Vader called before he turned to the dark side?

10. T B – Name the actress who left the Kabin to work as a dinner lady.

QUIZ FOUR

1. S B – Which actor has a tattoo on his arm that reads '100% Blade'?
2. J A and B P – Name the high-profile couple who tied the knot on July 29th 2000.
3. A F – What is the more common name for the complaint Tinea Pedis?
4. The W T C – What became the world's tallest building in 1972?
5. T O S S F M O G L F M – What were the first words spoken by Neil Armstrong when he set foot on the moon?
6. T H – Which famous comedian committed suicide in Sydney in 1968?
7. R R – Name the former Archbishop of Canterbury who died in the year 2000 aged 78.
8. The C of L – What is the emblem of Joan of Arc?
9. E P – Which fictional character was played on TV by Diana Rigg and on film by Uma Thurman?
10. S F – What was the name of the comic character played on TV by Bill Maynard whose catchphrase was 'Magic our Maurice'?

ANSWERS
1. Sean Bean 2. Jennifer Aniston and Brad Pitt 3. Athletes foot 4. The World Trade Centre 5. That's one small step for man, one giant leap for mankind 6. Tony Hancock 7. Robert Runcie 8. The Cross of Lorraine 9. Emma Peel 10. Selwyn Froggit

79

QUIZ FIVE

NAME THE TV STARS WHO CONNECT EACH GROUP OF THREE PROGRAMMES.

1. R G – *Casualty, Rhinoceros* and *The Grafters.*
2. M C – *EastEnders, Albion Market* and *Sunburn.*
3. D F – *Heartbeat, Yes Prime Minister* and *The Basil Brush Show.*
4. D K – *The Cuckoo Waltz, Foxy Lady* and *You Must Be The Husband.*
5. G H – *Coronation Street, The Royle Family* and *Keeping Up Appearances.*
6. M S – *The Liver Birds, Are You Being Served* and *That's My Boy.*
7. T S – *Home Sweet Home, Auf Wiedersehen Pet* and *Frank Stubbs Promotes.*
8. J A – *Z Cars, Last Of The Summer Wine* and *Coronation Street.*
9. G P – *Fairly Secret Army, Executive Stress* and *Butterflies.*
10. L B – *All Creatures Great And Small, Second Thoughts* and *Oxo TV ads.*

ANSWERS

1. Robson Greene 2. Michelle Collins 3. Derek Fowlds 4. Diane Keen 5. Geoffrey Hughes 6. Mollie Sugden 7. Timothy Spall 8. Jean Alexander 9. Geoffrey Palmer 10. Lynda Bellingham

80

QUIZ SIX

1. K S – Who won the Best Actor Oscar at the 2000 Oscar ceremonies?

2. L D – Which song title has provided a hit for David Bowie, Chris Rea and Chris Montez?

3. The L of the R S – What is the nickname of Japan?

4. D P – What is the title of the sitcom starring Richard Wilson that is mainly set on the River Thames?

5. The L D V – How were the Home Guard otherwise known during World War II?

6. The O W – What name was given to the 1840s conflict involving Britain and China?

7. P G – Who collaborated with Kate Bush on the hit single 'Don't Give Up'?

8. F M – Which literary villain was created by Sax Rohmer?

9. M of the R – Sally Carr was the lead singer of which chart-topping group of the 1970s?

10. D G – In a TV advert which footballer uttered the words 'Because I'm worth it'?

QUIZ SEVEN

1. G B – Who did Anthea Turner marry in the year 2000?
2. C H – What is the highest peak in the Chilterns range?
3. J L – Who won the Eurovision Song Contest in 1980?
4. The H that R B – What nickname is given to the New York Yankees baseball stadium?
5. L I A A – What is the title of the song written by Reg Presley that topped the charts for 15 weeks in 1994?
6. R S – Which magazine was first published in April 1967?
7. D R – What sport holds its major British events at a venue called Santa Pod?
8. L D – Vivian, Neil, Rik and Mike provided the backing vocals on which No. 1 hit?
9. The W G – What is the name of the local newspaper in EastEnders?
10. B D – Who shocked the world of boxing when he beat Mike Tyson in 1990?

QUIZ EIGHT

1. P and S – What was the title of the debut single for Hear'Say that shot straight to No. 1 ?

2. S F – In the film *Peter's Friends* who played Peter?

3. O S – What two words were spoken to gain access to Ali Baba's secret cave?

4. W R the W Y R – Which sporting competition was first contested in 1973?

5. K C – Who succeeded Yuri Andropov as the leader of the Soviet Union?

6. T L – Name the French painter who suffered the misfortune of breaking both his legs when he was a teenager.

7. B P – In the film *Independence Day*, who played the President of the United States?

8. A C D – Which author received a knighthood in 1908?

9. A H – Who did Rod Stewart marry in 1979?

10. G R – Crayford, Monmore and Walthamstow are all venues for which sport?

ANSWERS

1. 'Pure and Simple' 2. Stephen Fry 3. Open Sesame 4. The Whitbread Round the World Yacht Race 5. Konstantin Chernenko 6. Toulouse Lautrec 7. Bill Pullman 8. Arthur Conan Doyle 9. Alana Hamilton 10. Greyhound racing

QUIZ NINE

1. M S – What was the signature tune for the Glenn Miller Band?
2. R B – Who narrated the film *Zulu*?
3. T B – What was the name of Paul Shane's character in *Hi-De-Hi*?
4. L A G – Complete the following proverb – 'Great oaks from ----'.
5. C M – In the human body how is the gastronemius more commonly known?
6. Y T – Which non-league football team are nicknamed the Glovers?
7. The S of S – Which song starts with the line 'Hello darkness my old friend'?
8. P W A – What was the former name of Angola?
9. S D – Which gas is the chief cause of acid rain?
10. D B – Which famous name from the world of sport wrote his autobiography entitled '*White Cap And Bails*'?

ANSWERS

1.'Moonlight Serenade' 2. Richard Burton 3. Ted Bovis 4.'little acorns grow' 5. Calf muscle 6. Yeovil Town 7.'The Sound of Silence' 8. Portuguese West Africa 9. Sulphur dioxide 10. Dickie Bird

QUIZ TEN

1. R C B – How is Roy Vasey better known in the world of comedy?

2. D M – Which famous singer died on Christmas Day 1995?

3. A R – What post was held by Sir Martin Rees in the 1990s?

4. T H – Which familiar face on British TV designed the *Blue Peter* badge?

5. A M – Which actor, a highly decorated war hero, played himself in the film *To Hell And Back*?

6. C W – Who was appointed the US Defense Secretary in 1981?

7. N S – Who penned the play *The Odd Couple*?

8. The E of S – What title was taken by former British Prime Minister Harold Macmillan?

9. B P C – Who was the famous son of James Edward Stuart?

10. S C – Who was knighted on July 5th 2000, whilst wearing a kilt?

QUIZ ONE

....

NAME THE POP GROUPS FROM EACH SET OF THREE HITS.

1. The M S P – 'Australia', 'Everything Must Go' & 'A Design For Life'.
2. F and the D – 'Over You', 'I'm Telling You Now' & 'You Were Made For Me'.
3. E B the G – 'I Don't Want To Talk About It', 'Missing' & 'Walking Wounded'.
4. T F F – 'Woman In Chains', 'Mad World' & 'Shout'.
5. J K and the P – 'Shakin' All Over', 'Restless' & 'Hungry For Love'.
6. C K the C – 'Down To Earth', 'Misfit' & 'Ordinary Day'.
7. I M – 'Run To The Hills', 'Man On The Edge' & 'The Evil That Men Do'.
8. N K on the B – 'Tonight', 'Hangin' Tough' & 'If You Go Away'.
9. S R and the M – 'If You Can Want', 'Tracks of My Tears' & 'The Tears Of A Clown'.
10. O S C – 'The Circle', 'Better Day' & 'The Day We Caught The Train'.

QUIZ TWO

1. C C – Name the group that hit the charts in 1986 with the song 'I Just Died In Your Arms'.
2. C C – Who lived on Punchbowl Hill?
3. C C – Which was the only non-English team to win the FA Cup in the 20th century?
4. C C – Which actor played the only human member of the *Red Dwarf* crew?
5. C C – What do the initials CC stand for with regard to engine size?
6. C C – Who was the first ever BBC Sports Personality of the Year?
7. C C – Which supermodel became Mrs Richard Gere?
8. C C – What is the state capital of Nevada?
9. C C – On TV who partnered Mary Beth Lacey?
10. C C – What was the title of the 1937 film that earned Spencer Tracy a Best Actor Oscar?

QUIZ THREE

1. M F – Which horse won the Grand National in 1990?
2. S K – What is the name of the tiger in *The Jungle Book*?
3. K the G – Who is the best friend of Roland Rat?
4. F B – In the *Muppet Show* what is the name of the stand-up comedian?
5. H C – Which crustacean got its name from its habit of living in the discarded shells of snails?
6. B O O H – What is the title of the album that featured the songs 'Paradise By The Dashboard Light' and 'Two Out Of Three Ain't Bad'?
7. F the C - What is the name of the famous cartoon creation of Otto Mesmer?
8. K B – The name of which animal is derived from the Aboriginal meaning 'no drink'?
9. G S – What is the largest known invertebrate?
10. W S – What is the largest species of fish in the world?

ANSWERS
1. Mr Frisk 2. Shere Khan 3. Kevin the gerbil 4. Fozzie Bear 5. Hermit crab 6. *Bat Out Of Hell* 7. Felix the cat 8. Koala bear 9. Giant squid 10. Whale shark

QUIZ FOUR

1. M M – Which controversial rocker released the album *Anti-Christ Superstar*?

2. M M – Who won the Irish Peace Award in the year 2000?

3. M M – In an early series by Gerry Anderson who was the pilot of *Supercar*?

4. M M – Who topped the charts in the 60s singing about a Pretty Flamingo?

5. M M – Which famous man was born with the surname of Sigursteinnson?

6. M M – What is the name of the Leicestershire town famous for its pork pies?

7. M M – Who created and plays the character of Austin Powers?

8. M M – By what name is Derrick Evans known on TV when he dons a leotard?

9. M M – Which former lead singer of the Doobie Brothers had a solo hit with the song 'Sweet Freedom'?

10. M M – Name the record producer who founded the RAK record label.

QUIZ FIVE

NAME THE FILM FROM THE STARS WHO APPEARED IN IT.

1. A B T F – 1977 – Edward Fox, Dirk Bogarde and Laurence Olivier.

2. R B – 1968 – Ralph Bellamy, John Cassavetes and Mia Farrow.

3. B O – 1996 – Ewan McGregor, Stephen Tompkinson and Pete Postlethwaite.

4. A P to I – 1984 – Alec Guinness, Nigel Havers and Peggy Ashcroft.

5. C on S – 1966 – Bernard Bresslaw, Kenneth Williams and Harry H Corbett.

6. T M M – 1967 – Carol Channing, Mary Tyler Moore and Julie Andrews.

7. The P P S A – 1976 – Herbert Lom, Lesley-Anne Down and Peter Sellers.

8. The B of M C – 1995 – Meryl Streep, Annie Corley and Clint Eastwood.

9. The L G F – 1980 – Helen Mirren, Dave King and Bob Hoskins.

10. The B of the V – 1990 – Morgan Freeman, Bruce Willis and Tom Hanks.

QUIZ SIX

1. S S – Who won the Eurovision Song Contest singing in her bare feet?

2. S S – Who composed the musical *A Little Night Music*?

3. S S – What is the name of the disease spread by the tsetse fly?

4. S S – Who won an Oscar for her role as Sister Helen Prejean?

5. S S – What is the name of the famous prison in the city of New York?

6. S S – What name is given to the longest day of the year?

7. S S – The film *Sugarland Express* marked the big screen directorial debut of who?

8. S S – Which pop group's only Top 10 hit in the UK came in 1975 with a song called 'All Around My Hat'?

9. S S – Who married the newspaper executive Phil Bronstein?

10. S S – Who portrayed Margaret Thatcher in the TV drama *Thatcher: The Final Days*?

ANSWERS

1. Sandie Shaw 2. Stephen Sondheim 3. Sleeping sickness 4. Susan Sarandon 5. Sing Sing 6. Summer Solstice 7. Steven Spielberg 8. Steeleye Span 9. Sharon Stone 10. Sylvia Syms

QUIZ SEVEN

1. C F – Who lit the Olympic flame at the Sydney Olympics?

2. H C – Who became Senator of New York State?

3. C D – Who appeared on the back of a new £10 note?

4. F P – Who died on October 2nd 2000 aged 93?

5. E M – A 2000 newspaper headline read 'FAREWELL MR MISS WORLD'. Whose death was being reported?

6. B M – Who did Anita Dobson marry in the year 2000?

7. C C – In November 2000 which singer paid her ex-manager Johnathon Shalit a £2 million settlement?

8. J S – In December 2000 which *Coronation Street* star was admitted to hospital with knife wounds to his throat?

9. The N L C – In 2000 Helena Shovelton resigned as the chairman of what?

10. L of the O of the T – What title was awarded to Princess Anne in the year 2000?

ANSWERS
1. Cathy Freeman 2. Hillary Clinton 3. Charles Darwin 4. Fred Ponting 5. Eric Morley 6. Brian May 7. Charlotte Church 8. John Savident 9. The National Lottery Commission 10. Lady of the Order of the Thistle

QUIZ EIGHT

1. P P – Who was the boy that never grew up?

2. P P – What was the name of the professor who drove the Convert-A-Car in *Wacky Races*?

3. P P – In which American soap did Ryan O'Neal play Rodney Harrington?

4. P P – What was the name of the dinosaur mascot in the Saturday morning TV show *Multi-Coloured Swap Shop*?

5. P P – Which former presenter of Blue Peter went on to commentate on the sport of darts?

6. P P – What is the name of the fruity sounding suspect in the board game of Cluedo?

7. P P – What is the name of the father of Popeye the sailor man?

8. P P – Who painted a famous picture called *Guernica*?

9. P P – Who was the first husband of Anthea Turner?

10. P P – Which famous novel did John Bunyan begin writing whilst in prison?

ANSWERS
1. Peter Pan 2. Pat Pending 3. *Peyton Place* 4. Posh Paws 5. Peter Purves 6. Professor Plum 7. Poopdeck Pappy 8. Pablo Picasso 9. Peter Powell 10. *Pilgrim's Progress*

QUIZ NINE

1. J S – Which former world champion received a knighthood in the Queen's 2001 Birthday Honours List?

2. E M – Name the British yachtswoman who became the youngest ever female to sail solo around the world.

3. D E – What was the name of the widow of the screen cowboy Roy Rogers who died in 2001 aged 88?

4. L N – Which pop singer became an ambassador for the Brownies and Girl Guides in 2001?

5. G H – What is the name of the village near Selby which was the scene of a train crash in February 2001?

6. J M – Which actress took over the role of Clarice Starling in the 2001 film *Hannibal*?

7. S M – Who hosted the 2001 Oscar ceremonies?

8. U G – In March 2001 Michael Jackson was the Best Man at whose wedding?

9. D V V – What is the name of the Dutch doctor who was suspended from practice over his involvement in the Alder Hey Hospital scandal?

10. S R – Who wore the No. 1 bib at the 2001 London Marathon?

ANSWERS

1. Jackie Stewart 2. Ellen Macarthur 3. Dale Evans 4. Louise Nurding 5. Great Heck 6. Julianne Moore 7. Steve Martin 8. Uri Geller 9. Dick Van Velzen 10. Steve Redgrave